Toronto in 3 Days:

The Definitive Tourist Guide Book That Helps You Travel Smart and Save Time

Book Description

Don't waste time wandering around Toronto if you only have a few days to spend there! This book helps you with information about only the best and most popular sites to visit if you don't have a lot of spare time to spend in this wonderful city.

We give you the heads-up on the most interesting activities, including how you can best experience the local culture. We'll also give you accommodations and dining opportunities in all price ranges, so you'll know exactly what you're spending while you visit this beautiful, historic city. Toronto gives you experiences to fill your days and party away the nights, if that's what you'd like to do.

Most people do some shopping in town, and we let you know the best of the local marketplaces to browse in. We're not talking malls with department stores, but rather local shops that have many unique items for sale.

We'll also provide you with helpful information about getting to Toronto by plane, and then getting around by metro, cabs or buses. The currency is detailed, including the nicknames locals use for coins, so you know what they're talking about. Not sure when or how much to tip? We have you covered there, too.

National and local holidays and festivals are listed by date, in case you want to plan your short stay with an eye to attending a special event.

The People of Toronto

Toronto, Ontario, Canada has a population of nearly three million just in town, and over five million in the Greater Toronto Area. It's among the most multi-cultural cities you'll find, no matter where you have traveled. It's also a very safe place in which to spend a quick vacation.

Toronto residents speak more than 140 languages and individual dialects. More than 30% of Torontonians speak some language that is not French or English, at least in their homes.

The city of Toronto held about eight percent of the population of Canada in 2006, including 20% of all immigrants to Canada and 30% of the most recent immigrants. In fact about 1/2 of the population of Toronto was born outside Canada.

The top five most visible Toronto minority groups by percentage of population are:

- South Asian –+/- 12%
- Chinese – +/- 11.4%
- Black - +/- 8%
- Filipino - +/- 4%
- Latin American - +/- 2%

Language

Toronto is a tapestry of languages. The top five languages outside French and English that were mother tongues when polled in 2006 included:

- Chinese
- Italian
- Punjabi
- Filipino/Tagalog
- Portuguese

Diversity is also measured by the many languages spoken in the home. The non-official top languages spoken in the home are:

- Portuguese
- Spanish
- Italian
- Tamil
- Chinese

Culinary Delights

Toronto's cuisine reflects the size of the city, and its diversity. Different ethnic neighborhoods focus on their own cuisines, including:

- Chinese and Vietnamese cuisine in Toronto's SIX Chinatowns
- Greek cuisine on the Danforth
- Korean cuisine in Koreatown
- Indian cuisine in Little India
- Italian cuisine in Corso Italia and Little Italy

Other cuisines are found throughout Toronto, including:

- Hungarian
- Portuguese
- Caribbean
- Japanese

Toronto also has a sizable Jewish population, so you'll find Jewish delis and restaurants, and they adhere in various levels with kosher menu rules.

Holidays

National Holidays of Canada & **Ontario holidays

Holiday	2016	2017
New Year's Day *Jan-01*	Fri, January 1	Sun, January 1
Family Day** *Third Monday in February*	Mon, February 15	Mon, February 20
Good Friday *Friday before Easter Sunday*	Fri, March 25	Fri, April 14
Easter Monday ** *Government employees only*	Mon, March 28	Mon, April 17
Victoria Day *Monday before May 25*	Mon, May 23	Mon, May 22
Canada Day *Jul-01*	Fri, July 1	Sat, July 1
Civic Holiday** *First Monday in August* ** not an official stat holiday.*	Mon, August 1	Mon, August 7

Labour Day *First Monday in September*	Mon, September 5	Mon, September 4
Thanksgiving Day *Second Monday in October*	Mon, October 10	Mon, October 9
Christmas Day *Dec-25*	Sun, December 25	Mon, December 25
Boxing Day** *Dec-26*	Mon, December 26	Tue, December 26

Religious Beliefs

In Toronto, religion is a large topic. The city is among the most multi-cultural in all of North America. With so many cultures, one gets many religions. Toronto creates space for all religions, so that people of many beliefs can live together in harmony.

The most populous religion in Toronto is Christianity, and most Christians are Roman Catholics. The Anglican Church and United Church of Canada cover less than 10% of the residency of Toronto. The remaining religions of influence include:

- Islam
- Buddhism
- Judaism
- Hinduism
- Sikhism

Here is a quick preview of what you will learn in this tourist guide:

- Helpful information about Toronto
- Flying into the city
- Transportation tips in town
- Why Toronto is such a vibrant tourist spot and what you will find most remarkable about it
- Information on luxury and budget accommodations and what you'll get for your money
- The currency used in Toronto
- Tourist attractions you should make time to see
- Other attractions for entertainment and culture
- Events that may be running during your stay
- Tips on the best places to eat & drink for all price points, whether you want simple fare, worldwide dishes or Ontario flavor

Table of Contents

1. Introduction

The largest city in Canada, Toronto is an easy place to love. Within its orderly metropolitan area, you can shop, dine, explore, have fun or just kick back and relax.

The people of Toronto are friendly, and their ethnic diversity gives the city its vibrant feel. Since many of the activities and sites are found in the city's central area, you can see and do a lot, even in just a few days, without having to run until you drop.

A Brief History of Toronto

The city of Toronto is rich with history, and the people make it a great town. Its history is preserved, but it still holds its newfound modernity.

The area that is now Toronto was settled by Iroquois Indians thousands of years ago. Other tribes in the area included Huron, Seneca and

Mississauga. In the Huron Indian tongue, the translation of "Toronto" is "meeting place".

The French settled Toronto in the 1700's, but were driven out by the English, as hostilities between the two nations festered. Toronto officially became a city in 1793, originally called Fort York. It was the capital of what was then Upper Canada. The city was renamed "Toronto" in 1834.

Toronto has been a constantly growing business area since the middle of the 19th century. With ports and railways, it flourished. Through both World Wars, the city grew in investment and management areas. After World War II, the city saw even more growth.

By the early 1950's, Toronto's population was over one million and in the following years, the government was established and they created a subway system, and the people began moving to suburbs. The downtown area was still population-dense. By the late 1990's, Toronto officially became known as a mega-city.

Neighborhoods

The vitality and strength of Toronto's neighborhoods has led to the city being called (unofficially) a "city of neighborhoods". There are a staggering 140 neighborhoods, and we obviously cannot touch on all of them here. We'll hit the main areas you'll want to visit, though.

The center of the city is the most densely populated. It holds the hub of the city administration, and much of its business sector.

The suburbs East York and York are in the "inner ring" of Toronto suburbs. They have older homes, mostly middle-class residents, and the area is ethnically quite diverse.

The outer ring suburbs of Toronto include North York, Etobicoke and Scarborough. The "feel" more like suburbs.

What does Toronto Offer its Visitors?

What makes Toronto the thriving city it is? There are many contributing factors. It is among the most diverse, most vibrant, most livable and safest cities in North America. Some outsiders believe it has a high crime rate, but this is simply not the case.

Many city leaders the world over call their cities "diverse", but few actually fit the term as well as Toronto. If you've traveled in Europe, the people who share the train with you may be very similar. In Toronto, that's not the case. It's a bit like New York City in that respect. In any subway car or bus, you'll see multiple nationalities.

Ethnic groups have not all segregated themselves in Toronto, either. Outside of Little India, Koreatown and the Chinatowns, you'll find people of all nationalities living together. It's not like Chicago, where crossing a street takes you from one ethnic housing group area to another.

Downtown Toronto is vibrant, with a population in the tens of thousands, living in condominiums near the center of town. On an average weekend Toronto day, you can choose from 6-12 film festivals, music festivals, cultural events and food festivals.

You don't have to travel far to try different foods, either. You could go to Dundas Square for Brazilian food today, to Harbourfront tomorrow for spicy food, and on and on.

2. Key Information about Toronto

Money Matters

The official Canadian currency is the Canadian dollar. It is abbreviated as $CAD or C$, which helps in distinguishing it from other currencies that use the dollar, especially American currency.

The one dollar coin that is often used bears the image of a loon, leading it to be called a "loonie" by Canadians.

Coins are produced in these denominations:

- 5¢ nickel
- 10¢ dime
- 25¢ quarter
- $1 loonie
- $2 toonie
- You can still use pennies, but they are no longer minted.

Toronto Tipping

Canadians are famously polite, and this extends into tipping generously. Overall, Torontonians are good tippers.

Restaurant servers

Tipping is customarily 15-20%, depending on the food and the service. Bartenders are also usually tipped 15% if they provide good service.

Hotel staff

Hotels can be expensive, but not much of your room rate trickles down to the people who clean the rooms or run the front desk. $2-$5 a night is standard as a tip. Bellhops are generally tipped at $1-$2 for every bag they assist you with. Concierges are typically given 15% of the cost of any trip or event they hook you up with.

Restaurant Tipping

Gratuities are not usually included on your restaurant bills in Toronto. Most people in restaurants tip between 15% and 20%. If the service is poor, you may opt to pay less, and if it is exceptional, feel free to tip more.

If you're dining with a group, the restaurant will sometimes charge 15%-18% automatically for gratuity.

3. Transport to and in Toronto

Getting to Toronto by Plane

Toronto Pearson International Airport is Canada's busiest and largest airport. It handled nearly 41 million passengers in 2015. The airport is about 14 miles from the downtown area of Toronto.

The airport is a hub for Air Canada, Sunwing Airlines, Air Transat, WestJet and FedEx Express.

Getting to Toronto from the Airport

There are numerous ways to travel from the airport to Toronto. They include:

- Airport limos
- Airport taxis and minivans
- Public transit – Toronto Transit Commission
- UP Express (Union Pearson Express)
- Rental cars

Unless you are using UP Express to get to the city, allow extra time during normal rush hours of 6 to 9 AM and 4 to 7 PM. If the area has snow, allow an extra hour or more.

Airport Limousines

Time to Toronto: 30 - 60 minutes

Flat rate cost: $60 + tip

Airport Taxis and Minivans

Time to Toronto: 30 - 60 minutes

Flat rate cost: $55 + tip

Union Pearson Express (UP Express) Train

Time to Toronto: 25 minutes, from Pearson Terminal 1 to Toronto Union Station

Flat rate cost: $12.00 per adult one way

The UP Express connects Pearson International Airport with downtown Toronto. Trains depart every quarter hour from 5:30 AM until 1 AM. The trains offer plenty of space for luggage, power ports for each seat and free Wi-Fi.

Public Transit - Toronto Transit Commission

Time to Toronto: 60 - 90 minutes

Flat rate cost: $3.00 per adult

The Toronto Transit Commission (TTC) system provides bus service from about 5:40 AM until 1 AM. The buses run less frequently at night.

This is the least expensive way for you to get to Toronto, so it's quite popular with airport workers and locals. The drawbacks? They do not have luggage racks on buses or subways except for the 192 Airport Rocket bus. Drivers don't help passengers with bags. The TTC isn't ideal if you have much baggage. Of course, for a three day stay, this may not be an issue.

Toronto Cabs

Toronto taxis are part of Toronto's Ground Transportation Services, effective 5/3/2016. It includes limos and Uber vehicles. Toronto offers many taxis, at one single price, with no surging of prices. The taxis are very handy if you're in a hurry. The taxi cabs in Toronto are owned privately, not by the city.

Using owner-operated taxis, the owners can drive a maximum of 12 hours per day. Outside those hours, they can allow other drivers to use their vehicles. They may be affiliated with a taxi company, but they are not required to be.

All taxis can be operated 24/7, generally by operators who also rent out shifts. A GPS dispatch system is used to find customers for working drivers. Most customers contact cab dispatchers with their smartphones.

Payment and Tipping for Taxi's

Fares

Taxi cabs have a start fare of $3.25 to begin your trip. Additional charges are added depending on how far you are going. If you have more than four passengers, there is an additional person charge, at $2.00 for each person over four. Harmonized Sales Tax (HST) is already included in your fare. Typical tips are 15 to 20% of fare.

Taxi Colors

Correct at the time of publishing

Major Taxi Companies (Brokerages) in Toronto		
Name	Colour of Cars	Telephone Number
Beck	Orange/Green	416-751-5555
Maple Leaf	Blue With White Stripe	416-465-5555
CO-OP	Red/Yellow	416-504-2667
Diamond	Black/Orange	416-366-6868
Royal	Dark Blue	416-777-9222
Crown	Yellow	416-292-1212

Toronto Rental Cars

Toronto Pearson Airport has convenient car rentals on-site from well-known agencies, including Alamo, National, Hertz, Enterprise, Thrifty, Dollar, Avis and Budget. The counters are on Level One of Terminal 1 & Terminal 3 garages.

Public Transport in Toronto

Toronto subway service operates on weekdays and Saturdays from about 6 AM until 1:30 AM. Sunday service runs from about 8 AM to 1:30 AM.

On Christmas and New Year's Day, the subway runs start at about 9 AM. Holiday service for streetcars and buses will vary, so check the route schedule online before you leave.

Delays may occur in bad weather or due to traffic or construction delays. You can sign up for alerts from TTC that will inform you of any major disruptions in service.

4.Accommodations

Luxury Hotels - $431 to $519 USD per night and up

Your time in Toronto can be truly unforgettable if you spend the nights in a luxury hotel. They are located mainly downtown, in the Financial and Entertainment Districts, and in suburbs of the city. As you would expect, services and amenities are plenty, and the rooms are luxurious.

Park Hyatt Toronto – $519 USD per night and up

This is a popular destination, located on Bloor Street and Avenue Road, in Yorkville. It is in close proximity to the theater district, the Hockey Hall of Fame, Skydome, CN Tower, Stillwater Spa and Royal Ontario Museum, as well as tempting shopping venues.

Four Seasons Toronto - $474 USD per night and up

The Four Seasons Hotel soars 55 stories above Yorkville, which is the most glamorous restaurant and shopping quarter in Toronto. It offers spectacular design and well-defined sophistication. Floor to ceiling windows frame the Yorkville views and the streets with mansions in Rosedale nearby.

The Ritz-Carlton Toronto - $431 USD per night and up

The Ritz-Carlton overlooks the Toronto skyline and Lake Ontario. Guest rooms are 450 square feet and larger, some of the most spacious in town. Relax after check-in and sip a glass of one of their locally sourced wines.

Mid-Range Hotels in Toronto $216 to $300 USD per night and up

Not every traveler in Toronto wants to drop a lot of money on their accommodations. You can get very nice rooms and many amenities in mid-priced hotels, and save some bucks over the top-of-the-line luxury hotels.

The Windsor Arms Hotel – $300 USD per night and up

This hotel epitomizes bygone elegance in grand hotels. It has been a landmark in Toronto since 1927. Only recently re-opened, it is now a contemporary, stylish boutique hotel where celebrities often stay. The Windsor Arms has an aura of discreet elegance and luxury and an exceptional service level.

Thompson Toronto – $270 USD per night and up

The Thompson Hotel was designed by Studio Gaia of New York City fame. The rooms have full height windows with expansive views of Lake Ontario and the Toronto skyline. The boutique furnishings, hardwood floors and airy, open atmosphere create a comfortable place to rest after a busy day.

SoHo Metropolitan Hotel – $216 USD per night and up

The SoHo is sometimes called Toronto's finest hotel. You'll enjoy their spa treatments and their in-room technology, if you're in Toronto on business. Even if you're just staying for a few days, you'll enjoy the time you spend living the SoHo life.

Toronto Hotels for the Budget-Conscious $75 to $175 USD per night & up

What if you're ready to spend the days and nights seeing and doing everything Toronto has to offer? If you're not as concerned about the luxury of the hotel in which you're staying, there are still plenty of options for you, at budget prices.

Filmores Hotel – $80 USD per night and up

You'll find this hotel in the central Toronto core. It is only minutes from all the downtown highlights Toronto offers. The Filmores Hotel specializes in great service at budget prices, for travelers on short visits or extended stays.

Woodbine Hotel & Suites – $76 USD per night and up

The Woodbine is a basic hotel with lots of things to do, at a great value. They offer tennis courts, a hot tub and even a golf course. You'll enjoy the free Wi-Fi, free parking, business center and concierge services.

Hotel Victoria – $163 USD per night and up

This boutique hotel is found right in downtown Toronto. They offer modern guestrooms with new beds, modern custom furniture and hardwood floors. Located on Yonge Street, you're within easy walking distance of downtown attractions, shopping and dining. You're also mere steps away from ground and subway transit systems.

Airbnb's

For $28 USD per night, you can rent a bright and cheery great-room near the subway. At the other end of the price scale, if you need something ritzy, try a downtown mansion for $694 USD for a night.

The average price for a night at a Toronto BNB is $100. There are more than 300 rooms, apartments, homes and estates available in and around Toronto on Airbnb.com.

5. Sightseeing

There are so many things to do and places to visit in Toronto that you could never do everything in three days. That's where we step in, to show you the best way to spend your time, especially if you're only in town for a few days.

Chinatown

Chinatown offers an exciting tourist experience, with spas, historic monuments, activities, restaurants and shops. You could easily spend a whole weekend in Chinatown, but since you'll want to enjoy other parts of Toronto as well, you may want to make time for at least a half-day in Chinatown.

Aga Khan Museum

This is a museum of Muslim culture and Persian, Iranian and Islamic art. It was brought about by an initiative of the Aga Khan Culture Trust, which is an independent agency of the Aga Khan Network. It houses various collections of Islamic heritage and art.

CN Tower

This 1,815 foot tower defines the skyline of Toronto. The Canada National Tower is truly an iconic landmark, and ranks highly in Canada's most visited and celebrated attractions, and is even among the top tourist destinations worldwide.

Widely declared as a marvel of engineering, it's also an acclaimed dining and entertainment destination, with a restaurant on top. More than 1.5 million visitors visit the CN Tower every year, as they enjoy the breathtaking Toronto views. The elevator to the top has been unofficially proclaimed as the world's Number One elevator ride.

St. Lawrence Market

This marketplace is truly a piece of the history of Toronto. For each one of their 120 artisans, vendors and merchants, this marketplace is their one life's work. Their passion, pride and care help the market continue to thrive, 208+ years since it was first opened. You'll find many authentic food choices and you'll love the attention from shop-keepers who truly care about their unique wares and their customers.

6. Eat & Drink

You'll find many ethnic cuisine restaurants in Toronto, and it is also a place of fine dining establishments. You'll find a chef from Vietnam who creates and serves cerviche (a raw seafood dish) with yuzu (an Asian citrus fruit) and a fishmonger who remixes cured fish with okonomiyaki (a savory Japanese pancake).

But there is so much more! There are restaurants devoted to foods of early settlers of Canada, and Aboriginal Canadians. These are not gimmicky-styled establishments. Rather, they are affirmations that Toronto is continuing to grow, and is moving beyond traditional cuisine. There has never been a wider array of foods to devour than you can find in Toronto today.

The Toronto restaurants in our guide are classified into three price points:

Expensive Prices (over $76 USD)

Moderate Prices ($20 to $75 USD)

Inexpensive Prices (under $15 USD)

Sushi Kaji – Expensive

Chef Mitsuhiro Kaji creates his own soy sauce and has his fish flown in fresh daily from Tokyo. This ensures that he is using the highest in quality ingredients for his chef's choice (omakase) meals.

Toronto residents who live downtown will not normally trek very far for meals, and the fact that they will drive a half hour to get to Sushi Kaji shows that it has quality food and a very loyal following.

Canoe - Expensive

Canadian contemporary fine dining is the fare of the day every day at Canoe. It's found amongst bankers on the TD Centre's 54th floor, in the Toronto Financial District. Canoe has been one of the most acclaimed of Toronto restaurants for over 20 years.

Run by Olive and Bonacini, a Toronto restaurant group, Canoe showcases the best foods from sea and land, whether it's a tasting menu from Haida Gawii or Nova Scotia halibut.

Buca – Expensive

The Buca restaurants of Chef Rob Gentile have been beloved for years, and the newest addition is this Yorkville outpost. The menu focuses on seafood. But, rather than serving traditional salumi, Chef Rob creates a salumi di mare dish that is made with cured fish. You'll also find hand-made pizzas and pastas, but seafood is what most people rave about. This is the one place that just might be able to help your forget all about red meat.

Moderately Priced Restaurants

Bar Hop – Moderate

Craft beers bring most people to dine at Bar Hop. They have some of the finest in Ontario or Quebec. They have regular updates of their 36 taps. Quebec breweries make it onto the list sometimes, too, like Dieu du Ciel. This pub would be open even if they only offered craft beers, but they also offer pub fare foods like House Mussels and Vegan Cassoulet.

The Harbord Room – Moderate

You'll see all types of people dining at the Harbord Room, from elderly couples to tattooed Queen West chefs. They have superb service and excellent bistro fare. You must try their burgers if you make it there. The Harbord Room also has a popular bar, especially their drinks that mix booze and desserts.

Momofuku Daisho - Moderate

This is the Toronto brainchild of NYC Chef David Chang. He has a following in Canada, and people come from miles around to taste his fare. This is just one of Chang's Momofuku chain in the area of the Entertainment and Financial districts. Their specials include dry-aged beef ribeye and slow-cooked pork butt.

Inexpensive Toronto Restaurants

Jumbo Empanadas– Inexpensive

This stalwart of Kensington Market is among the city's favorite empanada makers. During the summer months, the patio facing the street is a great place to watch people while you enjoy Chilean pies by Irene Morales, the owner.

They have more than empanadas, too. They offer Latin delicacies like humitas, which is a tamale-like steamed dish, crafted with vegetables and mashed corn and wrapped in corn leaves.

Pho Hung – Inexpensive

Toronto is quite lucky to be home to many great Vietnamese restaurants, but very few have name recognition like Pho Hung. It is a popular restaurant, and a gateway to the vibrant Toronto neighborhood of Kensington Market. The service is not always cheerful, but the vermicelli dishes are tasty and inexpensive enough to keep diners coming back.

Takht-e Tavoos – Inexpensive

Downtown is not the locale of many Persian restaurants, and on the weekends, the lines for Takht-e Tavoos are very long. Relax – it's worth the wait! If you visit during the week, it's easier to get a table for late breakfast or lunch.

Among the favorite dishes is guisavah, made with eggs, walnuts and dates, with warm house flatbread, and kaleh pacheh, a classic, delicious Iranian breakfast.

7. Culture and Entertainment

Culture breathes life into a city. Toronto is alive and ambitious, continually being shaped and reshaped by the area's creative forces. That's what creates a feeling of belonging and a sense of place. It's also why Toronto is so attractive to locals and visitors alike.

Toronto is home for over 200 professional performing arts groups, 80 film festivals and opera, symphony and ballet companies that are recognized internationally.

Casa Loma

Casa Loma is the Spanish term for Hill House. It's a Gothic Revival house with gardens, found in midtown Toronto. Today it's a landmark and museum. It was built starting in 1911 and finished in 1914. Casa Loma sits at 460 feet above sea level.

Art Gallery of Ontario

Toronto's Art Gallery of Ontario has collections that include over 80,000 art works from the first century to today. The gallery has 480,000 square feet of space, and is among the largest galleries in North America.

High Park

This is a municipal Toronto park, spanning 400 acres. It offers natural beauty and recreation opportunities. It includes a zoo, playgrounds, gardens, and educational, cultural and sporting facilities. About one-third of the land in High Park has been left in its natural state, with an oak savannah ecology that is quite rare.

Toronto Entertainment

Canada's Wonderland

Canada's Wonderland is a whopping 330-acre theme park in Vaughn, Ontario, which is a suburb of Toronto, about 25 miles north of downtown. It was the first large Canadian theme park, and it's still the largest in the country.

This park has been the single most visited North American seasonal amusement part for years. It is open each day from May until September, and it is also open on some October weekends, too, to grab the last bit of summer fun before fall takes over.

Toronto Zoo

This wondrous zoo was founded in 1966 by Hugh Crothers, the first Chairman of the Toronto Metro Zoological Society. It opened for the first time in 1974, and was at that time called the Metro Toronto Zoo. It's owned by the city.

Covering 710 acres, this is the largest Canadian zoo. It has seven unique zoogeographic areas:

- Africa
- Indo-Malaya
- Tundra Trek
- Americas
- Eurasia
- Australia and
- Canadian Domain

Some of their animals are shown to the public in indoor tropical pavilions, or outdoors in environments similar to what they would naturally live in. There is viewing available for visitors at numerous levels. The zoo is open each day of the year, except for Christmas Day.

Black Creek Pioneer Village

Once called Dalziel Pioneer Park, this open-air Toronto museum lays southeast of the intersection of Steeles and Jane and west of York University. The name change reflects its location, overlooking Black Creek, which is a tributary of the Humber River.

Black Creek is a vision of what life looked like in rural Ontario in the 19th century. Schoolchildren in Toronto have frequent field trips to the village. The pioneer village was originally opened in 1960.

Toronto Night-life

As busy as Toronto is in the daytime, it's not hard to imagine how lively it is at night. The major Toronto venues are always hosting big touring acts, but the little clubs come out with some very talented musicians and groups, too.

N'Awlins

The Entertainment District of Toronto has frequently changed in the last 10 years, as consumer tastes and demands shift. However, N'Awlins club has been a favorite in that neighborhood for years. The success of N'Awlins involves offering live entertainment nightly, including jazz, blues and other music inspired by New Orleans.

Regardless of when you make it to N'Awlins, you are guaranteed to hear talented musicians. This venue also boasts a solid menu of tasty Creole-Cajun inspired dishes, including seafood jambalaya to fried alligator (yipes!) and Cajun calamari.

Rex Hotel Jazz & Blues Bar

The jazz scene in Toronto is definitely thriving, and right at the front you'll find the Rex. It has been in business since the late 80's. They have more great shows with local and world-renowned talent. The bar has a relaxed vibe and a minimalist décor. The dress code is definitely casual, so jeans are fine.

Grab yourself a beer and get ready to applaud all the musical sets. The Rex offers lots of free shows that bring jazz to very appreciative audiences in Toronto. The food is standard fare for pubs and they have decent prices on their drinks. Enjoy the patio in the summer months – it's divine.

Orchid Nightclub

Toronto is an optimal site for what may well be the next big wave in urban nightlife. That's not a surprise, since it's Canada's biggest city and home to a melting pot of art, culture and music.

Orchid is the embodiment of where the industry seems to be heading – the cocktails are unreal, the vibes are cool, the staff is professional and friendly. The service is amazing, the tastes are refined, the décor is super, the entertainment is incredible, and the prices are affordable. PLUS they don't have any attitude or smugness. They offer something for everyone looking for a night on the town.

8.Special Events in Toronto

Cavalcade of Lights – Saturday, November 26, 2016

Nathan Phillips Square is the location for the Cavalcade of Lights, an annual Christmas tradition. It's the first lighting of the official Christmas Tree of Toronto. Listen to live music by some of the top performers in Canada and enjoy skating parties on the outdoor rink and a spectacular fireworks show.

Toronto Christmas Festival at Harbour Front Centre - December 9 to 18, 2016

- More than 60 Vendors
- Polar Express Christmas Train
- Igloo Domes
- Entire Harbour Front Center full of activities
- 28 Live Bands & Christmas Carolers
- Musical Performances and Kids Shows

New Years Eve

There are so many wondrous events in Toronto every New Year's Eve! There is no shortage of options when you're ready to ring in the New Year, at whatever hotel, nightclub or lounge you choose.

New Year's Eve is undoubtedly the most epic, powerful party night in the year. It's a day and night devoted to debauchery and drinking, where everyone wants to gather to count out last year and sip their champagne as the ball drops. There are TONS of New Year's Eve parties in Toronto going into January 1, 2017, and you may have trouble deciding which one to attend, if you'll be in town at the end of 2016.

Winterlicious - January 27 to February 9, 2017

This is Toronto's favorite cold-weather celebration of culinary skills. It's a great opportunity to enjoy the culinary scene in the city through dinner and three-course menus being served at over 200 local restaurants.

Winterlicious offers you so many different experiences, including demonstrations, cooking classes, tastings & pairings, dinner theater, intimate dinners with famous chefs, and so much more!

"Doors Open Toronto" – May 27-28, 2017

These events are held all over the world, but Toronto's Doors Open event is one of the best. It gives you a chance to explore the buildings in Toronto and discover the unique story found behind the doors. This year you can see over 130 unique and memorable buildings in Toronto, and admission is free! Among the buildings open is City Hall, where you can check out the activities at the Information Center.

Canada Day - Saturday, July 1, 2017

Toronto celebrates Canada's birthday every year at Mel Lastman Square. The evening is free, and full of fun, with family activities, dance performances, live music and splendid choreographed fireworks shows with music.

Summerlicious – July 7 to 23, 2017

This is another famous culinary celebration in Toronto. It is held for two weeks in July, and it gives you a chance to savor three-course menus from over 200 of the top restaurants in Toronto. 24 new participants are being added in 2017, covering all types of food, from Asian fusion to Canadian.

Some of the top picks for Summerlicious 2017 include:

- Thailandaise Veal Pot Pie – made with spinach, Thai sausage and creamy polenta
- Galette de Sarrasin – a buckwheat crepe with farm egg, swiss cheese, spinach and arugula salad
- Northern Woods Mushroom and Thunder Oak Gouda Bannock Pizza - made with rocket greens, fried duck egg, mushroom and bolognese béchamel
- 6 ounce Filet of Beef Tenderloin - served with sauce béarnaise, potato pancake and summer greens

- Kefta Kebab – a juicy skewer of spiced Middle Eastern mixed beef and ground lamb
- Niagara peach semifreddo (semi-frozen dessert)
- Cornish Hen and Arkansas white sauce – served with hen broth and grilled cabbage
- Duck Confit Pappardelle - with truffle mousse, asparagus, patty pan squash, caramelized onion and mushrooms
- Crispy Oysters - with spicy cabbage cocktail sauce & sesame tartar
- The Ginger Scallion Noodle Bowl - with cabbage, shiitake and cucumber

9. Safety in Toronto

Toronto in many ways seems like the typical large city, but many have commented that is it quite safe, compared to large US cities.

Toronto was named the safest city of North America and the 8th safest city world-wide by the "Safe Index 2015" from The Economist Intelligence Unit.

Toronto does have SOME crime, just not a lot. If you stay around the touristy areas, you shouldn't have any troubles at all. If you like to explore, speak with your hotel front desk person to see if there are any areas you should avoid. When out walking, don't carry tourist guides or maps, as they may attract the wrong kind of attention.

The downtown area is home to panhandlers. If they approach you, be polite and just tell them "not today" if you don't want to give them any money. Some more serious money-seekers may try to stop you. Don't stop. They'll tell you a long story of woe and you'll fork over some money 15 minutes later, after their speech.

If you feel guilty not giving them money, please know that Toronto, and Canada in general, both have good safety nets for people who are truly needy. They can obtain any medicines, food and accommodation for FREE. They usually just panhandle for money they will use for drugs, tobacco or alcohol.

10. Conclusion

You'll feel welcomed in Toronto. It's the most culturally diverse city in the world. Many of the residents of Toronto were not born in Canada, but even with so many nationalities, they usually get along.

In good weather, you'll have a blast in Toronto. It's a big-time, vibrant city that is simply abuzz with warm energy. You can find world-famous restaurants, as you have seen, along with happening clubs and countless festivals.

Winter in Toronto is another story. Except for the Christmas to New Year's holiday celebrations, the streets are messy, with once-white snow efficiently plowed off the roads. Toronto gets about 48 inches of snow a year, and it does slow things down.

Patiently plan your short trip to Toronto in the spring, summer or fall. You'll have a great time. Toronto has an international buzz and the city really comes alive during the warmer months. Enjoy!

Printed in Great Britain
by Amazon

84323730R00037